SO OTHER PEOPLE
WOULD BE ALSO FREE

SO OTHER PEOPLE WOULD BE *Also Free*

THE REAL STORY OF
ROSA PARKS
FOR KIDS

Tonya Leslie, Ph.D.

Illustrations by Charnelle Pinkney Barlow

ROCKRIDGE PRESS

Interior and Cover Designer: William Mack
Editor: Mary Colgan
Production Editor: Kurt Shulenberger

Photography: page xi: Joseph Sohm; page 11: courtesy of Library of Congress, Prints & Photographs Division, FSA/OWI Collection; page 35: courtesy of the Kheel Center; page 48: courtesy of the US Department of Justice; page 63: Warren K Leffler; page 74: Cecil Stoughton; page 77: courtesy of Library of Congress, U.S. News & World Report Magazine Photograph Collection; page 78: Marion Trikosko; page 86: Angelo Cozzi; page 95: Johnny Silvercloud

Author Photo: Christina Morassi

Illustrations: © 2019 Charnelle Pinkney Barlow

ISBN: Print 978-1-64152-565-7 | eBook 978-1-64152-566-4

FOR YOUNG CHANGE-MAKERS
EVERYWHERE WHO STAND UP
FOR WHAT'S RIGHT AND FAIR.

CONTENTS

MONTGOMERY, ALABAMA, 1955

DECEMBER 1

Rosa Parks worked as a seamstress in a department store and regularly took the bus home from work. December was a busy time of year for her, as customers wanted a lot of work done before the holidays, and Rosa was distracted. But that work wasn't the only thing on her mind. Rosa had a second job at an organization called the NAACP.

The NAACP, which stands for the National Association for the Advancement of Colored People, was formed to protect black people against racial discrimination, brutality, and lynching. Black and white people in the South lived in a segregated and unequal world, and Montgomery, Alabama, in the 1950s was no exception. Often, black people were discriminated against, wrongly accused of crimes, jailed, and even killed. The people who worked at the NAACP actively fought for equal rights for black people and supported community members.

Rosa was the secretary for the local chapter of the NAACP, and she was thinking about the cases that she was helping resolve. There was a lot of work to be done, plus there were upcoming workshops and events that needed her attention. Her mind was so filled with these thoughts that she didn't even notice the bus driver that day. If she had, she never would have boarded that bus.

THE BUSES OF MONTGOMERY

Confrontations between black and white people on the segregated buses of Montgomery were common. Law separated black people from white people in public spaces. In practice, this

The restored Montgomery, Alabama, bus
Rosa Parks sat in on December 1, 1955

segregation was sometimes tricky to enforce, and the bus was an especially difficult place. The rule was that the first 10 seats on the bus were reserved for white people and the last 10 seats were reserved for black people.

Things were less clear about who got to sit in the middle of the bus, however. Technically, both black and white people could occupy these seats. But if a black person was sitting and a white person was standing, the black person was required to give up the seat. That wasn't all. Black and white people were not allowed to sit in the same row. So if one white person needed a seat, the entire row of black people had to get up. The bus drivers enforced these rules as they saw fit. Some drivers were cruel. Some even carried guns.

The driver of Rosa's bus that day enforced yet another rule of segregation: where and how black people could board the bus. Black people had to sit in the back of the bus but pay in the front. They would get on the bus, pay their fare, and then exit the bus to reenter through the back door. But some drivers would drive off before a passenger could get back on, leaving them stranded and out of money.

One day, many years earlier, Rosa entered a bus and noticed that the back was full. Rather than get off and try to push her way into the back, she moved to a space closer to the front. The bus driver insisted that she get off and enter from the rear. Rosa worried that no one would make space for her in the back and that the driver would take off before she could reenter. He spoke harshly to her, threatening to call the police if she didn't follow the rule. Eventually, Rosa exited the bus, and—just like she thought—the driver took off. The incident so upset her that from that day on, she avoided that bus driver whenever she could. She didn't want another confrontation.

SPARKING A MOVEMENT

On December 1, 1955, Rosa was consumed by her thoughts and wasn't paying attention. When the bus pulled up, she didn't notice that the bus driver was the same one she'd had a confrontation with before. She paid her fare and took a seat in the fifth row, which was the first row where black people were allowed to sit.

As the bus went along the route, it filled with white riders, and the bus driver demanded that Rosa and three other black riders give up their seats so the white riders could sit down. Rosa thought about the situation. She thought of all the times she had given up her seat. She thought about how she had been put off the bus once before. She thought about all the times she'd been treated unfairly just because of the color of her skin. She was tired of the injustice. She had a choice. She could comply, give up her seat, and everything would go on as it usually did. Or she could choose not to give in. She decided to stay seated.

Rosa's actions that day put into motion a series of events that would eventually become the civil rights movement. Her refusal to stand up would be followed by other bold acts, which would spark a movement that would change laws and the lives of black people across the nation.

Rosa's actions showed that sometimes being brave means taking a stand in the face of injustice. Rosa took a stand by sitting down. Her act of rebellion wasn't the first time she stood up for herself. In fact, she would later say that standing up for fair treatment was practically part of her DNA. It was how she was raised.

"EACH PERSON MUST LIVE THEIR LIFE AS A MODEL FOR OTHERS."

ROSA PARKS

Chapter One

ROSA'S EARLY YEARS AND CHILDHOOD

TUSKEGEE TO PINE LEVEL, ALABAMA

Rosa Louise McCauley was born on February 4, 1913, in Tuskegee, Alabama. Rosa's mother, Leona, was a teacher, and her father, James, a carpenter. The McCauleys had settled in Tuskegee because Leona hoped that she and her husband could secure work at the famed Tuskegee Institute, which would provide a stable income for the family and access to schooling for their children.

At the time, Tuskegee was considered a city of opportunity for black people. It was the home of the Tuskegee Institute, founded in 1881 by Booker T. Washington, a famous educator and speaker. Washington believed that black people would progress after the end of slavery by being educated and having economic opportunities in their communities. People wanted to go to his school because they believed it was the best place for black people to get an education. And they moved to Tuskegee to be part of the opportunity Washington spoke about.

Instead of seeking a job at the school, Rosa's father wanted to be a contractor because contracting work paid more money. Unfortunately, those jobs were hard to find. James would have to travel far to find work, leaving Rosa and her mother and brother alone in Tuskegee. So when Rosa was two years old, Leona decided to move with her two young children to Pine Level, a small farming community near the capital city of Montgomery, to be close to her parents and get the support she needed for her growing family.

Soon after the family arrived in Pine Level, Rosa's father left again in search of work. In order to support the family, Rosa's mother taught elementary school. The school where Leona worked was far from Pine Level, so she lived away from home during the week and returned on the weekends. Rosa and her younger brother, Sylvester, spent most of their time with their grandparents.

SEEING A BRAVE ROLE MODEL

Rosa's grandparents, Sylvester and Rose Edwards, were children when the Civil War ended in 1865. They were also both of mixed race. Rosa's grandfather grew up enslaved, and when he reflected on that time, he remembered never having enough to eat. He also remembered being treated harshly on the plantation after his father, who was the white owner, died.

As a result, Rosa's grandfather pushed against the laws of the time that said that black people and white people were unequal. He was also very outspoken. He would often call white men by their first name and not say "mister," which was how black people were supposed to address them. These kinds of actions were huge acts of defiance. As a black man, being outspoken could lead to arrest or even death. Still, Rosa's grandfather vowed that things would be different for his family, and he tried to protect them from the violence that was so prevalent at the time.

The Ku Klux Klan, a hate group known for terrorizing black families, was active throughout Alabama. They set fire to black churches and schools and killed many innocent black people. They wore white hoods to remain anonymous, so they could get away with their crimes.

Rosa's grandparents lived along a stretch of road that the Klan used often. At night, Rosa's grandfather would board up the windows and doors, nailing them shut from the inside. He would then stay up all night, a shotgun by his side, standing watch to protect his family from the Klan's nightly rides of terror. Often, Rosa stayed up, too.

TAKING A STAND

Rosa's grandfather was protective of his family and would not allow Rosa to play with white children. He knew they could sometimes be cruel to black children, and he wanted to shield Rosa and her brother from such abuses. Still, bullying was a daily occurrence. Sometimes, when a school bus filled with white children passed by, they would throw things at Rosa and the other black kids walking along the side of the road. The white children would say unkind things, too, trying to provoke the black children because they knew that if the black children talked back to them rudely, they could get in trouble.

One time, a white boy approached Rosa and threatened her. Rosa picked up a brick and said that if he even dared to hit her, she would throw it at him. After seeing Rosa stand up for herself, the boy walked away. When Rosa told her grandmother about the incident, she was scolded. The confrontation made Rosa's grandmother afraid. She knew that Rosa could get in trouble just for talking back to a white person, let alone

threatening one. But, Rosa didn't care. She told her grandmother, "I would rather be lynched than live to be mistreated and not be allowed to say, 'I don't like it.'"

To say she would rather be dead than live and be discriminated against was a courageous but dangerous statement. Mobs of white people routinely lynched black people. Yet Rosa decided she was always going to stand up for what was fair. Her early life of courage set the path for her later acts of boldness and bravery.

SEPARATE AND UNEQUAL SCHOOLS

Rosa's grandparents were the only black family in the Pine Level community who owned their land. The family owned 18 acres and raised chickens and cows. They also grew fruit and nut trees and tended their own vegetable garden. They lived off what they farmed and traded for whatever else they needed. When they finished working their own land, the family picked cotton on a nearby plantation. Everyone was expected to help on the farm and to pick cotton, including Rosa.

By the time Rosa was seven years old, she was working in the cotton fields. It was hard work, and everyone was expected to pick a certain amount each day. They worked from "can to can't"—or sunup to sundown—and most black children in Pine Level worked to support their families. As a result, the black schools were only open for about five months a year.

Rosa grew up in a loving home with a family that valued education. Since her mother was a teacher, she would teach Rosa at home when the school was closed or when Rosa was sick, which was often. But when Rosa did go to class, she noticed right away that there were two very different schools: the one available for black children, and the one for white children.

The black children went to a one-room schoolhouse where there was one teacher for about 60 students. The lone teacher taught grades one through six. She would call each grade, and the children would stand and learn their lessons in groups. The black community built and maintained the school. In the colder months, the bigger boys had to go out to cut wood to keep the wood stove burning so the students could stay warm. The windows had wooden shutters and were drafty.

The white children went to a new brick school that was paid for by taxpayers. Black people and white people both paid taxes equally, yet the money wasn't distributed equally. The white school had separate classrooms for each grade and was open nine months out of the year. Even though the white school was actually closer to her home, Rosa walked to the school for black children, which was farther away. White children rode in a school bus.

MOVING TO THE BIG CITY

When Rosa was 11, her mother decided that she should have better schooling, so Rosa moved to Montgomery and lived there with a family member. Montgomery was a big city compared to the small farming town of Pine Level and offered many more opportunities for education. There, she was enrolled in a private school called the Montgomery Industrial School for Girls. This large, three-story building was very different from the one-room schoolhouse Rosa had attended in Pine Level. The Industrial School was founded by two white women, originally from the Northeast. The women believed that black girls should have access to a strong education that taught the kind of self-sufficiency that Booker T. Washington called for. Not everyone shared this belief. In fact, the school was burned down twice, and the teachers were ostracized from the local white community for their beliefs about equality.

Still, Rosa learned a lot at the Industrial School. As well as academic subjects, she learned how to cook, sew, and take care of sick people. But perhaps the most valuable lesson she learned was that white and black people could get along and work together. This reinforced what she had learned from her grandfather—that she should

A sign at the Greyhound bus station in Rome, Georgia, 1943

be treated fairly, and, if given the opportunity, she could do anything just as well as anyone else.

SEEING SEGREGATION UP CLOSE

Montgomery was good for Rosa in many other ways. She had better access to health care, for instance, which was important because she was sickly as a child. And because Pine Level was such a small town, Rosa had mostly stayed close to home and didn't have much contact with people outside her family. In Montgomery, however, Rosa saw how segregation touched all aspects of daily life. There were separate public restrooms for black and white people. There were separate waiting rooms in the bus station. There were even separate public water fountains—one labeled for "Whites" and the other labeled for "Coloreds." Rosa often wondered if the water was different from the different fountains. Only later in life would she learn there was no difference in taste. Segregation didn't make sense, but it was the way things were.

Rosa also encountered segregation on public transportation for the first time. In Pine Level, people got around by walking or by riding in private cars. In Montgomery, people could get around on streetcars called trolleys. And, like most places in the city, the trolleys were segregated. Black passengers had to sit in the back of the trolley; white passengers sat in the front.

Rosa experienced a lot in Montgomery. At school, she learned that she could do anything she set her mind to. Outside of school, she learned that segregation meant black people were subject to daily assaults on their dignity. Eventually, Rosa would leave Montgomery—and school—but the things she learned there would propel her to find ways to make a change.

Segregation in the South

The first laws related to segregation passed in the South in 1865 and were called the Black Codes. In response to Congress passing the 13th Amendment abolishing slavery, Southern states enacted laws limiting black people's freedom. As black people asserted their independence, these state and local laws changed and became what are known as the Jim Crow laws. Jim Crow laws were very restrictive and remained in place until the Civil Rights Act of 1964. For 100 years after enslavement ended in America, black people were subjected to rules that restricted their movements, where they could live, and the access they had to certain services.

The following are actual laws from the Jim Crow era:

- It was illegal for white people and black people to marry each other.

- It was unlawful for a restaurant to serve food to black and white people in the same room unless separated by a wall, and there needed to be separate entrances.

- White and black children could not be taught in the same school, and in some states, they even received different textbooks.

Talk About It

Rosa's grandfather taught her to be bold, but the reality was that Rosa could get in serious trouble for standing up for herself. Standing up for yourself can be hard—and even dangerous. Do you think a person should always stand up for him- or herself?

Reconstruction After the Civil War

The years that immediately followed the Civil War and emancipation are called the Reconstruction era. The end of the war meant that there were a lot of issues that needed to be resolved. One issue was how to integrate the Confederate States that had seceded back into the Union. Another issue was how to integrate the newly freed black people into society now that the status of the former slaves had changed from "property" to citizen. As Black Americans began to make choices for their lives, reunite with loved ones, and acquire property, the Reconstruction era marked a period of remarkable self-determination.

A series of civil rights measures were passed to help protect the rights of the new citizens. For example, the 13th Amendment, passed in 1865, officially abolished slavery. Then the Civil Rights Acts of 1866 and 1875 gave Black Americans limited rights as citizens. Finally, the 14th Amendment, 1868, guaranteed citizenship to all Americans regardless of race. The government founded the Freedmen's Bureau in 1865 to distribute food and supplies and to establish schools throughout the South. However, much of this progress was met with brutal hostility as white Southerners resisted the gains.

Talk About It

The Reconstruction era must have been an extraordinary time for newly freed Black Americans. What might have been some of their most pressing issues?

"I WASN'T SCARED OR FRIGHTENED, BUT I WAS DETERMINED TO LET THEM KNOW I WAS NOT HAPPY WITH THE WAY I WAS BEING TREATED. UNDER SEGREGATION, YOU HAD TO PUT ASIDE YOUR DIGNITY... IT WAS VERY HUMILIATING. IT MADE YOU FEEL LIKE YOU WERE NOT BEING TREATED LIKE A HUMAN BEING."

ROSA PARKS

Chapter Two

ADULT LIFE AND EARLY ACTIVISM

A BUSY LIFE

There were no high schools for black students in Montgomery. So Rosa continued her schooling at a laboratory school at the Alabama State Teachers College for Negroes, a training school for teachers. She entered the 11th grade there but had to drop out. Her grandmother was sick, and Rosa had to return to Pine Level to care for her. After her grandmother died, Rosa's mother got sick too, and Rosa still couldn't return to school. Instead, she went to work to help out with family expenses. First she cleaned homes, and eventually she landed a job in a shirt factory. Rosa didn't mind taking the time to care for her family, but she would always dream about finishing high school.

Besides work, Rosa was active within her Montgomery church community and was a member of St. Paul African Methodist Episcopal Church (AME). She loved the hymns, and she enjoyed learning about the history of the church. It had been a place for prayer and worship for members of the black community since 1900.

Between working and caring for family, Rosa was busy. She didn't have time for romance. Then, one day, a young man named Raymond Parks—everyone just called him Parks—came to call on her. Parks was a barber in Montgomery, and his skin was so light that he could pass for white. At first, Rosa wasn't interested, but that didn't stop Parks. He would come by and take Rosa out for rides in his shiny red car. After a while, she began to look forward to their long rides and even longer talks.

BECOMING MRS. PARKS

Rosa learned a lot about Parks. He had lost both his parents at a young age—his father dying when he was just a baby, and his mother when he was a teenager. Rosa also learned that Parks never received formal schooling. He grew up in a white neighborhood but couldn't go to the white schools there, so his mother taught him at home. Despite his lack of formal schooling, however, Parks was a very smart man. He was interesting and involved in the community, and Rosa liked that he stood up for himself and others, especially black people. This reminded Rosa of her grandfather. She began to like Parks very much, and when Parks started talking about marriage, Rosa decided that she would like to marry him. In 1932, the two were wed in a small ceremony at Pine Level.

Parks encouraged Rosa to go back to school and get her high school diploma. This was a very big deal. At that time, very few black people had the opportunity to attend high school, much less graduate. According to the U.S. Census Bureau, in

1940, less than 10 percent of black people nationwide graduated from high school. In Alabama, the
number was even lower, only 3.9 percent. Rosa
went back to school and received her diploma at
the age of 20. It was a real accomplishment for
her and the realization of a lifelong dream. Still,
having a high school diploma did not give Rosa

the chance to find work that mattered to her. She kept doing the same menial jobs she did before.

ACTIVISTS!

Parks had a thorough knowledge of current events, and he was an activist. He saw a lot of the inequality and unfair things that were happening to black people in the South, and he worked closely with the local chapter of the NAACP to make changes in Alabama.

One of the cases that Parks was especially passionate about was the effort to free the Scottsboro Boys. The Scottsboro Boys were nine black teenagers, ages 13 to 19, who were falsely accused of assaulting two white women on a train near Scottsboro, Alabama. The teens didn't have good legal representation, and even though there was no evidence, all but one of the boys were convicted of the crime and sentenced to death.

Parks was part of a group of concerned citizens working to raise money to pay for a different lawyer so the teens could appeal the case. The group of activists held secret meetings late at night and in different locations, so they wouldn't arouse attention. Parks didn't include Rosa in these meetings and didn't tell her what was going on. Activists were often the targets of harassment and violence, and he wanted to keep her safe. Parks wanted to make sure that if Rosa was ever questioned about what happened at these meetings, she could truthfully say she didn't know.

Once, Parks held a meeting at their home. Rosa was there that night, and she saw the men sitting around a table with piles of guns. If anyone found out about these meetings, it could mean danger or even death. The men were armed in case they had to protect themselves. Rosa knew that Parks was an activist, and she knew that her husband's participation in these meetings could mean trouble for the entire family. But seeing all the guns on the table made Rosa realize just how dangerous things really were. She felt proud that her husband was willing to risk his life in pursuit of justice for others.

EXPERIENCING EQUALITY

Work was hard to find for Rosa, even with a rare high school diploma. Finally, she was able to land a job on the nearby Maxwell Air Force Base. She quickly saw that things were different there. Because the base was on federal property, racial segregation was banned in public spaces and on public transport. When Rosa was on the base, she sometimes would sit with white colleagues on the trolley. But once they got to the city, they would have to separate, and Rosa would have to move to the back of the city streetcar.

The daily practice of being segregated in some spaces but not in others made her even more determined to do something about the discrimination all black people experienced. She was tired of being treated like a second-class citizen and began to look for other ways to make a difference. She decided that one important thing she could do to help change things was to exercise her right to vote.

THE RIGHT TO VOTE

By law, black people had had the right to vote since 1870. The 15th Amendment said that no American citizen could be denied voting rights because of race, color, previous condition, or servitude. The reality, however, was different. Black people in the South were blocked from voting at every opportunity. Polling places were set up far away from black communities or changed at the last minute on Election Day. The requirements to register to vote were frequently changed, too. Black people had to pass a literacy test in order to register, and the questions were random and hard to prepare for.

Rosa knew that voting was important. Voting would allow black people to make choices about who their leaders were and who could help them achieve real equality. She decided that she would register to vote no matter how difficult it might be.

It took Rosa three attempts to get her voter registration card. When she first went to register, she had to take a test. She was told she passed it and that she would receive her card in the mail. The card never came. Rosa went back to register a second time and, again, took the test. This time, she was told that she had failed. When Rosa asked to see the results, she was refused. Finally, Rosa went back a third time to register to vote. She passed and was told that she would receive her card in the mail. Rosa was concerned, so she hand-copied all the answers to the test so she would have proof that she passed if her card didn't arrive. She didn't need the proof. This time, she received her card.

Receiving the card wasn't the end of the process, however. Rosa had to pay a poll tax. The poll tax was $1.50, and she was expected to pay not just for the year she registered, but for every year that she had been eligible and not registered! Rosa was 32 years old, and the amount came out to $16.50. That was a lot of money at the time. Still, Rosa paid the money and cast her vote. Being registered to vote was a big deal, and Rosa took it seriously. Her husband had tried to register but was never able to successfully do so in

Alabama. Rosa would exercise her right to vote in every election in her lifetime.

Registering to vote and getting her high school diploma were hard-won victories. Still, Rosa knew that they weren't the only solutions to the inequalities all around her. She was tired of the different rules that were applied to black people, and she was fed up with the acts of violence and intimidation that black people faced when they stood up against injustice.

FROM OUTRAGE TO ACTION

Life was becoming more challenging for black people in Montgomery. Black soldiers were returning from fighting in World War II. Many activists hoped that by fighting to defend American democracy for all, black soldiers would gain access to the rights they had been denied. But that wasn't the case. Returning black soldiers were not treated with respect, and many found that they weren't even able to register to vote.

Rosa's brother, Sylvester, had just returned from fighting in the war, where he served as a medic and cared for wounded soldiers. He had served with distinction. Yet upon his return to Alabama, he was spat on and was unable to find work. Eventually, Sylvester grew tired of waiting for things to change in the South and moved his family north to Detroit. Rosa knew things had to change and decided it was time for her to engage in public activism.

JOINING THE NAACP

Rosa joined the NAACP in December 1943 and became one of the first female members of the Montgomery chapter. When she went to her first NAACP meeting and paid her membership dues, she was the only woman in attendance. The men needed a secretary, and Rosa started taking notes. After she became secretary, she kept records of member meetings, kept track of member registrations, and, most importantly, tracked reported incidents of racial discrimination. She also became an advisor for the youth council and worked to desegregate the public library. There was a library that was open to black people, but it had limited funds and resources. Rosa wanted that library to have all the right resources. Unfortunately, the youth council was not successful in its attempts, but they kept on fighting.

But joining the NAACP was risky. Because of the success the organization had in fighting segregation, many white people felt it was a radical group, and known members were at risk of losing their jobs, being harassed, or facing vigilante violence.

WAITING FOR THE RIGHT MOMENT

Things were changing across the South, but they were not changing fast enough. Boycotts and protests were happening around the country, and the Montgomery chapter of the NAACP was paying close attention, looking for a model of action to follow.

In 1953, for example, a bus boycott in Baton Rouge, Louisiana, took place when the city council voted to raise the bus fare. The increase angered black people, who made up 80 percent of bus riders. They were angry not only because the bus fare went up, but also because they were still subjected to the rules of segregation. Paying more to sit or stand in the back of the bus, even if the seats reserved for white people were empty, wasn't right. And even though a new seating law was passed, it was not enforced. Eventually, a citywide bus boycott was organized. The boycott lasted about four days, and a new agreement was reached in regards to seating on the bus. The boycott helped change the rules, though it did not help end segregation altogether. Still, it was encouraging. Activists in Montgomery thought the Baton Rouge boycott could be a model for something even bigger locally.

The Power to Vote

The 15th Amendment, which was ratified in 1870, stated that "The right of citizens of the United States to vote shall not be denied or abridged by the United States or by any State on account of race, color, or previous condition of servitude." This amendment gave black men the right to vote (women weren't given voting rights until 1920). Despite this, for decades, the right to vote was systematically suppressed in many states through acts of violence and intimidation by white supremacist groups. Often, these groups consisted of white governing officials, which meant there was no way for black voters to appeal.

Without the power to vote, black people would not be able to get their voices heard. They would not be able to vote for candidates who supported laws to protect their interests. Eventually, Congress enacted the Civil Rights Act of

1957, the first federal civil rights legislation to be passed since 1875. This allowed black people to register to vote without intimidation or unfair tests. Securing the ability to register to vote and then to vote safely became a key part of the civil rights movement.

Talk About It

Protecting people's rights and ability to vote safely is an ongoing issue. Today, there are still concerns about voter suppression and voter fraud. Why is it important to protect voting rights?

The NAACP

The National Association for the Advancement of Colored People (NAACP) is a civil rights organization that was formed in 1909 by black and white activists to support Black Americans in their fight for justice. One of the NAACP's key initiatives was the anti-lynching campaign. After the Civil War, white supremacist groups used lynching as a way to intimidate Black Americans. Most of the people who were lynched were black, and the white people who committed these murders were rarely convicted—even when their crimes were known in the community. Besides lynching, the NAACP focused on other initiatives to end race-based discrimination. Local chapters of the NAACP sprang up across the United States to support these efforts. Today, the NAACP works to secure educational and economic equity and still fights to eliminate race-based discrimination.

Talk About It

Rosa was aware of the protests and boycotts that were happening around her. Are you aware of protests and boycotts that are happening in or around your community? How can you learn more about what is going on in your community?

People picket against the F. W. Woolworth
Company's practice of segregation, April 20, 1963

"NO, THE ONLY TIRED I WAS, WAS TIRED OF GIVING IN."

ROSA PARKS

Chapter Three

ROSA SITS TO TAKE A STAND

ENCOURAGING CHANGES

Things were changing across the nation in the mid-1950s as the practices of segregation were being dismantled. One year after the Baton Rouge bus boycott, the U.S. Supreme Court decided that racial segregation of children in public schools was unconstitutional. Up until that time, the laws held that black and white children could be taught in "separate but equal" schools. In the landmark case *Brown v. Board of Education of Topeka*, the court ruled that separate educational facilities were not equal at all. Schools had to be desegregated. White groups opposed school integration and made it difficult for black children to enter previously all-white schools. Still, black activists were encouraged and realized that the idea of desegregation could be expanded to other areas.

The tide was turning nationally, but things in Montgomery, Alabama, remained the same. Segregation on buses continued to be a big problem, and there were almost daily confrontations between white bus drivers and black passengers.

CONFRONTATIONS ON THE BUS

In 1955, two teenage girls were arrested for refusing to give up their seats. The first teen, Claudette Colvin, was returning home from her segregated high school and was sitting on a bus with her friends. They all sat in a row—two were on the right side and two on the left. A white passenger stood in the aisle between them, so the bus driver demanded that the teens give up their seats. Three of the students got up, but Claudette remained seated. She felt it wasn't fair. Because of the tricky laws of segregation, black and white people could not sit in the same row together. Even though there were now seats available, the white passenger still couldn't sit down unless Claudette vacated her seat, too.

The bus driver drove over to a police car, and the officers boarded the bus and asked Claudette why she wouldn't give up her seat. Claudette was defiant. She said that it was her right to sit. But the police got rough. They pushed her books out of her lap and handcuffed her. She was then taken to the adult jail instead of the juvenile detention center. As Claudette waited for her mother to arrive to bail her out, she was scared. Even after she was released from custody, Claudette and her family worried that they or their home could be attacked. Claudette was the first person arrested for challenging Montgomery's bus segregation laws.

Rosa and other activists learned about Claudette's arrest while they were discussing how to organize a citywide boycott of Montgomery's buses. They wanted to find the right incident to use as a test case to take legal action to push for desegregation of the buses.

Several months later, another teen, Mary Louise Smith, was arrested for refusing to give up her seat to a white female passenger. She was arrested and charged with failure to obey segregation orders. Her father bailed her out. The incident was kept quiet, known only to family and neighbors.

Organizers worried that neither of these cases was the right one to inspire a widespread protest. Activists and organizers were looking for someone who was willing to test the laws of segregation and live in the spotlight as the public face of the protest. This person needed to have a positive public image and a clean reputation. Rosa knew about the organizers' attempts to find the right face of the boycott. She also knew of the two young women who had been jailed for refusing to give up their seats on the bus. But the day she decided not to give up her seat wasn't premeditated. She didn't plan to protest beforehand. It's just the way things happened.

ROSA SITS TO TAKE A STAND

On Thursday, December 1, 1955, Rosa boarded the city bus after a long day at work. The holidays were coming up, which meant it was a busy time at the department store where she worked. Most of the business came in between the Thanksgiving and Christmas holidays, so Rosa had been busy keeping up with work. She was also working for the NAACP. There were cases that she was working on, and she was organizing a workshop. She had a lot on her mind. So much so that Rosa didn't notice that the bus driver that day was the one she usually avoided. That driver's name was James Blake.

Twelve years earlier, Rosa had experienced an incident on the bus that shook her so much she didn't even tell her husband. Rosa entered the bus and paid her fare. She was then supposed to exit the bus and reenter through the back door. But the bus was crowded. Rosa worried that if she tried to get in through the back door, there wouldn't be enough space for her. She also worried the bus driver would leave her as she had seen other drivers do in the past. And that's exactly what happened. From that day forward, she would refuse to board the bus if she saw James Blake driving. Instead, she would simply wait for the next bus to arrive.

However, on December 1, Rosa didn't notice James Blake at the wheel of the bus. She paid her fare, entered, and took a seat. As the bus went down its usual route, it began to get full. A white passenger entered the bus and stood in the aisle, as black passengers occupied the seats in the middle row. James told Rosa and three other black passengers to give up their seats for the white passenger. Even though only one white passenger needed a seat, all four black people were required to move because it was illegal for black and white people to sit in the same row.

Rosa shifted in her seat so the other passengers could move and give up their seats, but she stayed seated. She refused to follow the bus driver's demand.

This was a bold move. By staying seated and refusing to obey the law, Rosa staged a

nonviolent protest. It was considered an act of civil disobedience. Once the driver realized that Rosa was not going to move, he called the police. The people on the bus grew quiet as they wondered what would happen next.

ROSA'S ARREST

When the police arrived, Rosa asked, "Why do you all push us around?" The police officer said, "I don't know, but the law is the law, and you're under arrest." The police officers took Rosa to city hall. Once there, she asked to make a phone call, but she was not allowed. Then she was taken to the city jail. There, she was fingerprinted, and her mug shot was taken. Rosa wasn't afraid, but her husband and her community were very concerned. Rosa was well known in the community. Everyone thought of her as a kind person who went out of her way to help others. The fact that she had been arrested just for sitting on the bus made everyone pay attention. They worried that she would be beaten or worse.

Rosa's husband and friends sprang to action. They helped secure a lawyer to make sure Rosa was treated fairly. They also secured the bail money needed to get her released from jail. When she was taken to jail, she was charged $14. She was then released on $100 bail. While it was a fairly peaceful confrontation, Rosa was still annoyed by the injustice of it all.

Rosa was free, but her arrest marked a turning point. Activists began to wonder if Rosa was the case they had been waiting for. She was well respected in the community. She had graduated from high school, which was rare for a black woman in Montgomery. She was also a registered voter. Rosa would be the perfect person to be the face of an organized protest—if she would agree.

Brown v. Board of Education

Brown v. Board of Education of Topeka was a landmark 1954 Supreme Court case. The ruling in the case established that racial segregation in schools was unconstitutional. It overturned a previous ruling that made segregated facilities legal as long as the facilities for white and black people were equal.

Prior to this ruling, schools for black and white children were, indeed, separate, though anything but equal. In this famous case, a man named Oliver Brown filed a suit against the Board of Education in Topeka, Kansas, because his daughter was denied entrance to the all-white elementary school. In the lawsuit, Brown argued that segregation violated a clause in the 14th Amendment. The clause said that states had to provide individuals with "equal protection" under the law. Four other cases of school segregation combined under the *Brown v. Board of Education* case, and finally, the Supreme Court decided that "'separate but equal' has no place." Segregated schools were seen as "inherently unequal." The ruling was critical because it began the dismantling of the practice of segregation in public spaces.

Talk About It

Laws ended the legal segregation of black and white people in public spaces, but the practice of segregation took longer to end. Can you think of current examples where there are practices that don't match the stated rules? Why might it be hard to change behaviors to meet new rules?

School Desegregation

As black students began to integrate schools, they were met with protests. Sometimes these protests turned violent. There are many famous stories about black children integrating schools, but Ruby Bridges's story is among the best known.

Ruby Bridges was six years old when she attempted to integrate the all-white William

U.S. marshals escort Ruby Bridges from school

Frantz Elementary School in New Orleans. To ensure her safety, she was escorted to school and then back home by four U.S. marshals. At first, there were protests when Ruby arrived at the school. She spent the first day in the principal's office to avoid the chaos. Eventually, the protests died down, and parents allowed their children to go to school with Ruby. Still, Ruby's family suffered for their decision. They lost jobs, received death threats, and were otherwise harassed. Nonetheless, Ruby said there were many other people who supported her. The image of Ruby walking to school is the subject of a famous painting by Norman Rockwell called *The Problem We All Live With.*

Talk About It

Ruby's father was reluctant to send her to integrate the school alone. Her mother was nervous about it but felt that it was important. Do you think you would have been courageous enough to integrate a school, like Ruby Bridges, in order to end the practice of segregation?

"YOU MUST NEVER BE FEARFUL ABOUT WHAT YOU ARE DOING WHEN IT IS RIGHT."

ROSA PARKS

Chapter Four

THE BUS BOYCOTT

A COURAGEOUS DECISION

Rosa's family was worried. If Rosa became the public face of the protest against segregation, she could be putting herself in harm's way. At first, her husband, Parks, was against it. He worried that Rosa would become a target for bullies and the Ku Klux Klan. He had protected his wife from his own activist work for so many years. But ultimately, Rosa decided to do it. She knew that she was making a sacrifice in order to push for change, and she decided it was worth it. Parks supported Rosa in her decision. He promised to protect her.

Once Rosa agreed, things moved quickly. A mass protest was scheduled for the upcoming Monday morning. Many local organizations, including the Women's Political Council (WPC), had been preparing for just this moment. They began to develop and hand out leaflets to inform the community about Rosa's situation and the upcoming protest. The leaflet told the story of the ongoing confrontations on the bus. Rosa was yet another woman who had been targeted by bus drivers and arrested by police. Black people were urged to protest this unfair treatment by refusing to ride the buses the following Monday. This would show bus companies that their behavior would not be tolerated.

The leaflets encouraged black people to find alternate routes to school or work, and if they couldn't do that, they should avoid going to school or work altogether. Word about the boycott spread quickly over the weekend. Still, it was a time of great uncertainty for the organizers. What would happen next? Would people stay home? Would black people really stay off the buses? Would this boycott change anything?

Monday was a tense day. Somehow, news about the boycott was leaked to the local newspapers. As bus drivers prepared to take their routes, they were escorted by police officers on motorcycles. The police were there to keep the peace. But they didn't have anything to do. The buses were mostly empty.

THE COURT CASE AGAINST ROSA

On the Monday of the boycott, Rosa did not take the bus to work as she usually did. Instead, she went to court. When she arrived at the courthouse, there was a crowd waiting for her. They yelled words of encouragement. Her husband was right—now everyone knew who she was.

James Blake, the bus driver, appeared in court, as did a witness. The witness said that Rosa was being unreasonable and that there was a seat she could have moved to. That was untrue.

Still, the court found Rosa guilty of violating the segregation laws and fined her. But because she was found guilty, her lawyers would be able to appeal the decision to a higher court. This was the moment the organizers had been waiting for.

After court, Rosa headed to a local church. Community leaders were gathering to discuss the boycott and figure out next steps. Reverend Martin Luther King Jr. was selected to speak, and what he said electrified the crowd.

"And you know, my friends, there comes a time when people get tired of being trampled over by the iron feet of oppression. There comes a time, my friends, when people get tired of being plunged across the abyss of humiliation, where they experience the bleakness of nagging despair. . . . And we are determined here in Montgomery to work and fight until justice runs down like water, and righteousness like a mighty stream."

After King spoke, Rosa was introduced to the crowd. Anyone who didn't know her before definitely knew her now. Then a three-page resolution was shared that asked everyone to stay off the bus until a fair settlement was reached with the city. The organizers were asking for three conditions to be met in order to end the boycott:

1. Courteous treatment of black passengers generally.

2. No black person would be forced to surrender their seat to accommodate another rider. No one would have to stand over an empty seat.

3. The bus company would employ more black drivers on the routes.

Initially, these conditions were not about ending the segregation laws. Instead, they were about getting better treatment for black passengers. Still, the city officials would not agree to these conditions. It was decided at the church meeting that the boycott would continue, though no one dreamed it would last 381 days.

The organizers worked hard to find alternate ways to get black people around the city. Shared-ride services sprang up to transport black passengers to a variety of locations, and donations came in from across the nation to help support the shared-ride system. The money paid for gas and insurance and for the traffic tickets that piled up against the drivers.

As the boycott went on, it proved to be a financial hardship for the city. Ridership on the buses was low, and the bus companies were losing money. Businesses along bus routes were losing money, too. Since there were no bus riders, there was no traffic to their stores. The bus boycott was bankrupting the city, and everyone wanted it to stop, but city officials weren't yet ready to negotiate.

Instead, city officials looked for ways to end the bus boycott and disrupt the shared-ride system. For example, city police began ticketing and arresting black drivers for a variety of phony charges, like driving too fast or too slow. Some were charged with failing to stop at stop signs, and some were charged with stopping too long at stop signs. One driver received 17 tickets! Officers would also arrest black people who gathered at informal pickup locations. They were accused of "loitering." Despite these efforts, the shared-ride system continued and supported the transportation needs of black riders for more than a year.

City officials looked for more ways to disrupt the boycott, and they began to target Rosa and other organizers. On February 21, 1956, a Montgomery grand jury indicted 89 bus boycott organizers, including Rosa and Martin Luther King Jr., for violating a 1921 law that barred boycotts without "just cause." Rosa was photographed being fingerprinted by the police. Of the 89 people indicted, only King went to trial. He was found guilty, fined $500, and sentenced to one year of hard labor. An appeals court later overturned this decision.

As the city brought lawsuits against the boycott organizers, the activists were pulling together their own lawsuits to push for changes in the law related to segregation. Boycotts and protests alone were not going to be enough to create systemic change. The laws had to change as well, to ensure social transformation. It would be one of these lawsuits that eventually ended the bus boycott, and it would be led by women.

THE CASE FOR DESEGREGATION

Four women who had been separately confronted on city buses brought together a federal case, bypassing the state courts, to challenge the Alabama state and city laws requiring segregation on buses. Though Rosa had also been arrested for violating the segregation laws, it was decided that she would not take part in this case. She had her own legal case pending—the appeal—and the lawyers agreed to use multiple strategies to advocate for legal changes.

The case of the four women became known as *Browder v. Gayle.* And on June 5, 1956, when the court decided in favor of the women, segregation on Alabama's buses officially ended. The city and state immediately appealed the decision. So while King and other officials celebrated the legal victory, they continued the bus boycott until the appeal could be heard.

The final decision didn't come until December 20, 1956. And on that day, U.S. marshals formally served the court's orders to Montgomery's city officials, ending segregation on the buses. King officially ended the 381-day boycott when he said, "The year-old protest against city buses is officially called off, and the Negro citizens of Montgomery are urged to return to the buses tomorrow morning on a non-segregated basis." The next day, the Montgomery buses were integrated, and the boycott was over. King and other leaders, including a white boycott supporter, boarded a bus and posed for photos while sitting in seats previously reserved for white people.

Rosa also posed for a picture that signified the end of bus segregation.

This approach of mobilizing people to public action while also pursuing legal action was at the heart of the civil rights movement. The boycott was a visual symbol of black people's willingness to go to great lengths to demand the respect and dignity they deserved. But the boycott alone was not responsible for changing the laws that supported the structures that held segregation in place.

The Civil Rights Movement

Rosa Parks is often called "the mother of the modern-day civil rights movement" because her actions sparked an ongoing effort for Black Americans to gain equal rights under the law. Between the 1950s and 1960s, black people staged boycotts, sit-ins, and other types of protests in their attempts to change laws to end segregation and other unfair practices. One example of success occurred on September 9, 1957, when President Eisenhower signed the Civil Rights Act of 1957 into law. This law made it illegal to prevent anyone from voting, allowing Black Americans to register to vote without facing intimidation or unfair tests.

One of the most famous events of the movement was the March on Washington in 1963. The goal of the march was to advocate for legislation that established job equality for everyone. There, Martin Luther King Jr. gave his famous "I Have a

The March on Washington for Jobs and Freedom,
August 28, 1963

Dream" speech. The peaceful march brought together more than 200,000 people of all races.

Talk About It

The civil rights movement was an act of social justice. Social justice is based on the idea that all people have the equal right to fairness, health, well-being, and opportunity. Battles for social justice are still fought today—all around the world. Can you think of any social justice issues happening in your community?

"*I WOULD LIKE TO BE KNOWN AS A PERSON WHO IS CONCERNED ABOUT FREEDOM AND EQUALITY AND JUSTICE AND PROSPERITY FOR ALL PEOPLE.*"

ROSA PARKS

Chapter Five

LIFE AFTER THE BOYCOTT

AN ANGRY RESPONSE

The bus boycott was over. Life was different in Montgomery. Things had changed. But many people were not happy with the changes, and violence erupted around the city. Snipers shot at the integrated buses. Four Baptist churches were bombed. King's house was bombed. Other activists' houses were bombed, too. The white people who were sympathetic to the boycott were threatened and harassed, and many left town, fearing for their lives.

Over the year-long bus boycott, Rosa was active and visible in the movement. She not only participated in the bus boycott but also donated money to the shared-ride system, and she supported various organizations in the work they were doing. Throughout, Rosa was not immune to the negative sentiments. As she became more involved, she became more of a target. Just like her husband predicted, things got intense.

The backlash to Rosa's participation in the movement was quick. First, her husband was harassed at work until he finally left his job. Then Rosa lost her job at the department store; she was told her services were no longer needed. Then their rent was raised. On top of all this, there were the threats. Rosa's phone rang at all hours with threatening callers, and threatening letters came regularly. When Rosa walked outside, she was often recognized and confronted.

Rosa also faced hardship within the activist community. Some people involved in the movement were jealous of the attention she received, and they began to exclude her from organizing work. Rosa and Parks were struggling financially and personally.

Rosa had to think about her choices. Was it safe for her to stay in Montgomery? Life was becoming too dangerous. The couple had no income coming in, and she and her husband were unable to find work. Her mother was sick, and the constant harassment was taking a toll on everyone. Rosa decided that the best thing she could do for her family was to leave. So she moved her family to Detroit to live with her brother.

LIFE IN DETROIT

Life in Detroit wasn't any easier. Starting in the early 1900s, many black people left the South and moved away to cities like Detroit, seeking better opportunities. This would later be recorded in history as the "Great Migration." Because so many people migrated to Detroit, there was a lot of competition for jobs and housing. And though Detroit wasn't officially segregated, black and white people settled in separate neighborhoods. As new homes were constructed, black people found that they were not allowed access to certain homes or neighborhoods. Eventually, protests erupted. Rosa had left the problems in Montgomery only to find a whole set of new ones in Detroit.

Finding work was difficult for Rosa and Parks. Eventually, Rosa accepted a job out of state on a historically black college campus in Virginia.

Rosa enjoyed her job as the hostess of a guest-house at Hampton Institute. She met all the interesting and important guests who came to the university. It was a beautiful campus, and Rosa was well respected by the university community. Ultimately, being so far away from her family took its toll, and Rosa went back to Detroit. While she was away, her husband obtained a barber's license and got a job. He also registered to vote for the first time. Rosa found work, too, as a seamstress. It wasn't a lot of money, but it was steady work.

CONTINUING THE STRUGGLE FOR CIVIL RIGHTS

Meanwhile, the civil rights work in Montgomery continued. Rosa spoke at events on behalf of the NAACP nationwide and was active in local neighborhood groups. She and Martin Luther King Jr. stayed in touch, and she supported his actions in Montgomery, which included joining one of his groups called the Southern Christian Leadership Conference (SCLC). The group was organized to help coordinate the local protest groups throughout the South. Rosa attended SCLC conventions and retreats whenever she could.

As King was gaining prominence as a black leader, he became more and more committed to using nonviolent resistance in order to bring about social change. The nonviolent movement included strategies like boycotts and sit-ins, and many organizations adopted these strategies. Nonviolence was also King's personal philosophy. He felt that it was better to win over an adversary through friendship than through intimidation.

King didn't practice self-defense. Throughout all the violence that was perpetrated against him and other leaders, including the bombing of his home, King remained committed to a nonviolent approach. He felt that he had to stay focused on the injustices of segregation, not the perpetrators of the injustices. Rosa experienced this firsthand when she attended an SCLC convention in Birmingham in 1962. King was making his closing remarks when a white man in the audience rushed the stage. He hit King several times. Instead of shielding his face, King looked directly at the man and spoke to him softly. Later, he refused to press charges against the assailant. Rosa thought it was extraordinary that King's commitment to nonviolence meant that he wouldn't defend himself physically, no matter the risk.

THE NONVIOLENT MOVEMENT GROWS

Meanwhile, the nonviolent approach was catching on. Segregation laws were being tested in all areas of life and across the South. In one important example, students from Greensboro, North Carolina, sat in at a segregated lunch counter. Though they were refused service, they continued to sit as part of a nonviolent protest. This set off a series of sit-ins where black and white students would sit at lunch counters in an attempt to desegregate them. The community response to these protests was often violent in nature, however. The nonviolent protesters were heckled, spat on, and in other ways treated aggressively. Still, the student protestors retained their composure, often reading books or just sitting quietly, refusing to leave. These quiet demonstrations gained media attention, and over time, the lunch counters were desegregated.

These student demonstrators in North Carolina formed the Student Nonviolent Coordinating Committee (SNCC) in 1960, and organized their own protests and tactics. The SNCC played a big role in many of the major events in the civil rights movement, including the establishment of freedom rides. Freedom Riders, as they came to be called, were black and white activists who rode interstate buses throughout the South, challenging local laws against desegregation. Like so many other nonviolent demonstrators, the Freedom Riders were often the target of violence from the local communities.

CONTINUED ACTS OF VIOLENCE

Though many people adhered to the nonviolent approach, many more resorted to violence, particularly those who opposed King's message. King's house was bombed multiple times, and King was even stabbed. Innocent people were targeted and killed, too. For example, in 1963, four girls were killed when the 16th Street Baptist Church in Birmingham was bombed. The four girls were getting ready for Sunday service when the bomb went off. The response in the hours and days following caught national attention and added to the mounting sympathy toward the civil rights cause. All across the South, much of the violence against peaceful protestors was captured on TV and witnessed by the nation.

Several laws and rulings came as a result of the national outcry, changing the country forever. President Lyndon B. Johnson signed into law the Civil Rights Act of 1964, which ended segregation in public places and banned employment

President Lyndon B. Johnson signs the 1964 Civil Rights Act as Martin Luther King Jr. and others look on

discrimination. A year later, Johnson signed into law the Voting Rights Act of 1965, which further enforced the 14th and 15th Amendments. Many states in the South used a lot of different measures to keep black people from voting, including intimidation tactics and violence. It took Rosa three attempts to finally get to vote, and her husband was only able to register to vote after they moved to Detroit. The Voting Rights Act was a big deal because it meant states could no longer deny the right to vote based on literacy tests, nor could states change their voting laws whenever they wanted. Though the laws changed, it would take years to change hearts and minds. In many ways, this is still happening today.

Rosa knew that her commitment to the civil rights movement had to be ongoing, and she remained active in all aspects of her community by helping with organizations that supported schools as well as those that supported voter registration. Eventually, Rosa got a job as an assistant to John Conyers Jr., the U.S. representative for Michigan. She started in 1965 and remained until she retired in 1988. The job was steady and offered her a pension and health insurance, and it also allowed her to continue her activism work.

White Resistance, White Response

Many white people violently resisted the civil rights movement. Some white politicians and elected officials were firm segregationists and were bold in denouncing desegregation efforts. One such well-known person was Theophilus Eugene "Bull" Connor.

Bull Connor was an Alabama politician who believed strongly in maintaining segregation. He often allowed violent acts against peaceful protestors. For example, in 1961, he allowed a white mob to attack a group of Freedom Riders with pipes. The Freedom Riders were integrated groups of college students who rode buses together throughout the South to challenge segregation laws. In another instance, Bull allowed the fire department to use high-pressure fire hoses against peaceful protestors. Many of these images were televised. In many ways, the public outrage against these images served to help create social change.

Segregationists protesting the integration
of schools in Little Rock, Arkansas, 1959

Talk About It

*Television played a key role in the civil rights
movement. The news coverage showed the violent
response against activists and peaceful protestors
and caused many people to take positive action.
Does social media today play a role in moving
people to positive action? If so, how?*

Martin Luther King Jr., 1964

Martin Luther King Jr.

Martin Luther King Jr. was a Baptist minister and activist who became a leader and spokesperson for the civil rights movement. He is best known for advocating for a nonviolent approach, and his tactics were used throughout the movement. King led the Montgomery bus boycott and helped organize other nonviolent protests throughout Alabama. He is also known for his speeches, including his most famous "I Have a Dream" speech, delivered at the 1963 March on Washington. In this speech, King speaks about his vision of equality, saying, "I have a dream that one day, right there in Alabama, little black boys and little black girls will be able to join hands with little white boys and white girls as sisters and brothers." Sadly, he didn't get to see that dream. He was assassinated on April 4, 1968.

Talk About It

Would you say that King's dream has come true today? Why or why not?

"I WOULD LIKE TO BE REMEMBERED AS A PERSON WHO WANTED TO BE FREE . . . SO OTHER PEOPLE WOULD BE ALSO FREE."

ROSA PARKS

Chapter Six

THE LIFE AND LEGACY OF ROSA PARKS

THE BEGINNING OF THE END?

In many ways, Rosa's refusal to get up on the bus in 1955 sparked the civil rights movement. Her brave act incited a boycott that ultimately changed laws in Montgomery and throughout the United States. But when did the civil rights movement end? Many, including Rosa, would probably say it never ended; it just changed.

By 1967, many laws had passed giving black people legal protection and equal rights. Still, attitudes didn't change overnight, and many of the new laws were not embraced or enforced. Discrimination, though against the law, was still widely practiced, impacting the lives of Black Americans in a variety of ways. For example, housing discrimination meant that many black people did not have access to new developments that were going up, or they were charged higher rents to live there. As a result, most black people still lived in segregated communities. And when black people tried to integrate white communities, white homeowners often would leave. This became known as "white flight." Discrimination also affected hiring practices. Unemployment rates for Black Americans were high. Black people were denied access to jobs that would provide a steady and stable income.

Another tension of the time was the strained relationship between black communities, which were still largely segregated, and the police force, which was mostly white. Many charged the police force with being aggressive and abusive to black people. These tensions erupted in the summer of 1967 when more than 100 riots broke out across the United States. Many of the riots began as a response to aggressive and abusive policing practices. As black communities protested against the police, these confrontations often led to violence, property destruction, and even death. Riots occurred in cities such as Atlanta, Chicago, and Birmingham, as well as in Detroit, Rosa's home.

RIOTS IN DETROIT

In Detroit, black community members found it difficult to secure the money and official paperwork necessary to own and operate nightclubs. Black people were not welcome in white-owned clubs, so many created their own unofficial clubs where black people would be welcomed. The local police aggressively raided these spaces, shutting them down and issuing fines. The black community felt that these clubs were unfairly targeted. It was an ongoing tension.

Then in July 1967, Detroit police raided a club in the black community, and the community protested angrily. Things escalated quickly. The governor requested help from the federal government, and soon 2,700 Army paratroopers arrived in the city. For five days, the city was in turmoil. People were hurt, and properties were destroyed. There were conflicting reports about who was responsible. In the end, about 7,200 people were arrested, 1,200 people were injured, and 33 people were killed.

Rosa lived near where the uprising took place. She had friends who were injured in the riots and saw firsthand the damage being done. Her family suffered personally, too. Parks's small barbershop was destroyed, and all of his tools were stolen. When he tried to protect his business, Parks was harassed by the police. Rosa understood the desperation and frustration that fueled the rioting. She knew that people were only trying to move forward and the discrimination they experienced provoked violence. Still, she felt that this type of violence ultimately hurt the entire civil rights cause.

1968: A TRANSFORMATIVE YEAR

Loss continued to follow the movement. In April 1968, Martin Luther King Jr. was assassinated in Memphis, Tennessee, where he was planning a protest against low wages and poor working conditions for sanitation workers. His assassination shocked the world and sparked riots in more than 100 cities nationwide. More buildings were burned. More people were injured. And many activists worried that without King's leadership, the movement would not continue.

Yet the work had to go on. After the assassination, Rosa was called in to continue the work that King had started in Memphis. She worked with his wife, Coretta Scott King. Together, they tried to keep the momentum going, even though people were discouraged. Still, Rosa tried to stay optimistic. When she attended King's funeral, she met other people who were committed to keeping the movement alive, including Democratic presidential candidate Robert F. Kennedy.

Robert was the brother of President John F. Kennedy, who had been assassinated in 1963.

American sprinters Tommie Smith and John Carlos protesting racial discrimination at the 1968 Summer Olympics

Robert Kennedy opposed racial discrimination and had been working with King on issues related to human rights and social justice. People were hopeful that if Robert became president, he could advocate for more changes. The moment of hope was short-lived. Robert Kennedy was assassinated in June 1968.

Meanwhile, change kept coming across the nation. At the 1968 Olympic Games, Tommie Smith and John Carlos, gold and bronze medalists in the 200-meter run, brought global attention to the movement. While standing on the awards platform, they raised their black-gloved fists in what was commonly known as the "black power" salute. There were other protests happening as well. Students of all races opposed the United States' involvement in the Vietnam War, and large-scale anti-war protests spread across the country. Many black leaders (including King) supported the anti-war efforts. These overt political acts were widely criticized. Still, they brought the conversation about the rights of Black Americans into a global spotlight.

Though much was happening in the late 1960s, racial oppression didn't go away. New leaders suggested new approaches to address the ongoing social problems affecting black people. Rosa, too, remained active in the movement, addressing problems that continued to plague her community. For example, in the 1970s, she organized efforts to support the freedom of political prisoners. One case Rosa was particularly involved with was the case of Joan Little, a black woman who was accused of murdering a white prison guard in North Carolina. Joan said she acted in self-defense as the guard was assaulting her. Rosa helped raise money to support the case, and Joan became the first woman in the United States to be acquitted of murder on the grounds of self-defense.

Throughout the 1970s, Rosa continued to work for Representative John Conyers Jr. in his congressional office in Detroit, and she spent a lot of her free time supporting her community. She volunteered her time, teaching women how to sew, working with children, and advocating for voter registration. The decade was also a tough time emotionally for Rosa, who suffered several personal losses. In 1977, both her husband and her brother died of cancer within months of each other. Then in 1979, her mother died, too.

By the 1980s, Rosa found herself alone without immediate family. She rededicated her life to the movement to secure rights and opportunities for the black community. She was older now, but she continued worked with Conyers until she retired in 1988. Even after retirement, she never stopped working and speaking out to support the causes she believed in. She donated most of her money to charity and lived a quiet, humble life.

HER LEGACY

Rosa Parks went from private activist to a public face for a movement. She is most often remembered for taking a stand by staying seated on that Montgomery bus. But that was just a moment in the life of a woman who was, and continued to be, committed to securing equality and justice for others. But Rosa also suffered because of those actions. She was plagued by the hateful mail and threatening comments of people who wanted to diminish her accomplishments—people who wanted to silence her.

Yet to the end of her life, Rosa was an activist, and her work for social justice was constant and steady. She advocated for voter registration, volunteered her time to a variety of court cases, and worked with neighborhood children. In 1987, Rosa established her own organization. The Rosa and Raymond Parks Institute for Self Development was an afterschool program that taught children to always strive for their highest potential and never lose their dignity.

While Rosa worked in the Conyers office, she was often visited by people who wanted to commend her for her life's work. Even so, Rosa was never concerned with getting accolades for her work and role in the civil rights movement. Her participation was eclipsed by other figures of the movement. It would take 24 years after the bus boycott for the NAACP to recognize Rosa's achievements, and often, when she was recognized, people limited her accomplishments to that historic moment on the bus.

In the 1990s, Rosa began to get recognized for the fullness of her life and the steadiness of her determination. In 1990, a bronze sculpture of her was displayed at the National Portrait

Gallery in Washington, D.C. In 1993, a Rosa Parks Peace Prize was created. In 1996, Rosa received the Medal of Freedom, presented by President Bill Clinton, and in 1999, she became the 121st recipient of the highest civilian award bestowed by the U.S. government: the Congressional Gold Medal. Still, she remained humble. To Rosa, it was never about the fame—it was always about the work. It was always about the people.

Rosa Parks passed away of natural causes on October 24, 2005, at the age of 92.

Her coffin was brought from Detroit to Washington, D.C., where she became the first woman and second Black American to lie in honor in the Capitol Rotunda. It is estimated that more than 50,000 people came to honor her.

At her funeral in Detroit, many people spoke of her achievements. They talked about her kind heart and humble spirit. They reminded everyone of the legacy she left behind. Perhaps the words of President Barack Obama (who was then a senator from Illinois) best sum up Rosa's mark on the world: "The woman we honored

IT IS THIS SMALL, QUIET WOMAN WHOSE NAME WILL BE REMEMBERED LONG AFTER THE NAMES of SENATORS and PRESIDENTS HAVE BEEN FORGOTTEN

— Barack Obama —

today held no public office, she wasn't a wealthy woman, didn't appear in the society pages. And yet when the history of this country is written, it is this small, quiet woman whose name will be remembered long after the names of senators and presidents have been forgotten."

Rosa Parks's legacy continues.

The Struggle for Justice—Today

The civil rights movement has evolved, and there are movements today that still advocate for and address the civil and political rights of black people. One contemporary movement is Black Lives Matter, which speaks out against racial inequality within the criminal justice system.

Social justice activists work to maintain equal rights and opportunities for *all* people. There are social justice advocates who fight for women's rights, children's rights, and the rights of any and all people who may be discriminated against anywhere in the world. Like the leaders of the civil rights movement, the leaders of today's movements face challenges. Not everyone agrees with the work being done, or people simply resist—often violently—the changes these movements

A Black Lives Matter protest

promote. Still, the work of supporting, promoting, and securing the rights of all people is critical to our world.

Talk About It

Can you think of other social justice advocates today or in the past? Who were they advocating for? What rights were they protecting?

FURTHER READING

WEBSITES

archive.org

historyforkids.net/rosa-parks

makers.com

naacp.org

pbs.org/black-culture

womenofthehall.org

BOOKS

Bridges, Ruby. *Through My Eyes*. New York: Scholastic Press, 1999.

Freedman, Russell. *Freedom Walkers: The Story of the Montgomery Bus Boycott*. New York: Holiday House, 2006.

Olson, Lynne. *Freedom's Daughters: The Unsung Heroines of the Civil Rights Movement from 1830 to 1970*. New York: Scribner, 2002.

Parks, Rosa, Haskins, James. *Rosa Parks: My Story*. New York: Dial Books, 1992. Print.

Rubin, Susan Goldman. *Brown v. Board of Education: A Fight for Simple Justice*. New York: Holiday House, 2016.

INDEX

Note: page numbers in **bold** indicate photos

ABOUT THE AUTHOR

Tonya Leslie, PhD, is a writer, researcher, and educational consultant. She is passionate about children's books. She is also passionate about fighting for social justice. She lives in Brook-  lyn, New York, with her dog, Basha. More information about Tonya can be found at TonyaLeslie.com.

CPSIA information can be obtained
at www.ICGtesting.com
Printed in the USA
LVHW022134270819
629091LV00002B/2

9 781641 525657